STEMscopes™
CA-NGSS 3D

STEMscopedia – Second Grade
ISBN: 978-1-64168-875-8

Published by Accelerate Learning Inc., 5177 Richmond Ave, Suite 1025, Houston, TX 77056.

To learn more, visit us at www.stemscopes.com.

10 9 8 7 6 5 4 3

00220201030

This STEMscopedia is designed to be used as a companion piece to our online curriculum.

EXPLAIN	**STEMscopedia** A reference material that includes parent connections, technology, and science news

Only STEMscopedia pages are included in this book, and directions on how to use these pages are found in our online curriculum. Use the URL address and password provided to you by your district to access our full curriculum.

STEMscopedia - Second Grade
Table of Contents

Mapping Our World

STEMscopedia

Have you ever wanted to go somewhere but did not know how to get there? How did you find the answers?

Maps show us where things are in the world. If you wanted to look up what state the Grand Canyon is in, you could find it on a map. A map also shows us the different shapes and kinds of land and water in an area.

Using a map, we can find places such as mountains, rivers, and canyons. What makes them so special, and why are they on a map?

They are different kinds of landforms. What other kinds of landforms can you think of? How could you identify them on a map?

What is a landform?

A *landform* is a natural structure on Earth's surface. Most landforms are formed slowly over millions of years. They form Earth's *geography*, or physical features.

Scientists who study geography are called *geographers*.

Landforms are always changing, but maps do not change as often. Why is this?

The Grand Canyon is a 277-mile gorge in northern Arizona. In some places, the canyon is a mile deep!

Most changes happen so slowly that you would never notice them without special tools. Scientists use these tools to make very precise measurements over long periods of time.

STEMscopedia

What are different types of landforms?

Landforms come in different shapes and sizes. Four common landforms are mountains, hills, valleys, and plains. You can use certain characteristics to identify each type.

- *Mountains* are large landforms made of rocks that are steep (rise quickly) and have a point at the top. Some mountains are so tall that the tops are covered in snow all year—even during the summer!

- *Hills* are landforms that are similar to mountains. Hills are not peaked on top. Instead, hills have soft, rounded tops. They are made of grass, dirt, and rocks. Hills are not as tall as mountains.

- *Valleys* are low areas between two mountains or hills. A valley can be large or small, depending on how far apart the mountains or hills are.

- *Plains* are the flattest landforms and can be very large. The Great Plains of the United States stretch from the Mississippi River to the Rocky Mountains. The panhandle area of northern Texas is also a plain.

STEMscopedia

What are the different bodies of water?

Bodies of water come in different shapes and sizes. Oceans, lakes, rivers, and streams are a few examples. You can use certain characteristics to identify each type.

- *Oceans* are large bodies of water. You cannot usually see land on the other side of an ocean because of its size. Oceans contain salt water.

- *Lakes* are also bodies of water, but they can be big or small. They are usually smaller than most oceans. Most lakes hold fresh water, but some lakes have salt water in them. All lakes are surrounded by land on all sides. Sometimes you can see the land all the way around the lake. A *pond* is similar to a lake, but it is much smaller.

- *Rivers* flow through many valleys. The Rio Grande River runs through the Rio Grande Valley in Texas. As water runs through the valley, the valley can become wider and deeper over time.

- *Streams* are similar to rivers, but they are much smaller in size. Since some streams are not very deep, they may dry up after long periods without rain.

STEMscopedia

How can we represent landforms and bodies of water?

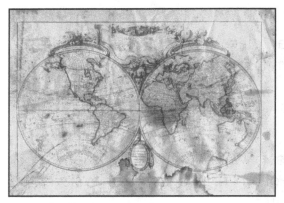

This map is from the 1800s.

Some common ways to show information about landforms and bodies of water are *maps*, *globes*, and other *models*.

Many famous explorers used maps to draw what they found in a new area. They used many details, such as landforms and bodies of water, to make sure they could come back to that place again. Others used maps to write down information they learned from space exploration.

There are different kinds of maps that are used for different things:

Physical Maps: A physical map is used to show where different landforms and bodies of water are located. Physical maps are colored to show where mountain ranges are, and they look like they are popping up off the page. They are very useful for geographers who want to study landforms and bodies of water.

Aerial Maps: An aerial map shows what something looks like from above. They can be images from a satellite or drawings done by hand. This aerial map was created using a computer program. Can you tell where the mountains are? What other landforms do you see?

Topographic Maps: This type of map uses lines to show the different heights of hills and mountains. They also show how deep a valley, ocean, or river is in an area. Many hikers and travelers rely on these maps for information.

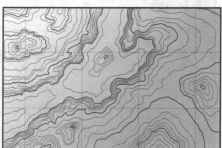

STEMscopedia

Globes allow people to see what the entire world looks like. Many globes include each of the continents in one color and the water in another color. Some globes also have raised markings to show different landforms, such as mountains or hills. They are shaped like a sphere to allow us to look at the world on a smaller scale.

Both of these globes use different colors to show the land and the water. Some globes use blue to show where the oceans are.

Scientists create physical models of different landforms. They can use this information to reenact a volcanic explosion or other natural disaster. They can show what an area looks like now to compare it to a map from long ago. Some museums use models of landforms to teach others about them. Some students make models using clay to show what an area looks like. There are many uses for models of landforms and bodies of water.

This model shows an island with mountains. It shows how high or low different areas are. The blue areas are the lowest and the red areas are the highest.

STEMscopedia

Naming Landforms

Take a trip with your child to a local national park. If you do not live near one, find another scenic area where there are at least two landforms of the types studied in this lesson, such as hills and valleys. Be sure to bring along a notebook and crayons or colored pencils.

Make sure to ask the park rangers for a map of the park. Review the map with your child, noting places where the specific features of the area are named for landforms (e.g., Davis Mountains, Rio Grande Valley). Discuss with your child how place names can give information about the types of landforms in an area.

While at the park, ask your child to identify the types of landforms you both observe, including bodies of water. After identifying each type of landform, ask your child to create a drawing of the landforms and the bodies of water in the notebook. Be sure to label the drawing as a mountain, hill, valley, plain, or lake. You may wish to ask questions, such as:

- How do you know that landform is a hill and not a mountain? (How do you know that landform is a mountain and not a hill?)

- (if you are in a valley) What is the shape of the valley? Do you see a river? Do you think a river or a glacier was the main shaper of this valley?

Forms of Water on Earth

STEMscopedia

Reflect

Emma just played outside all afternoon. She is hot and tired. She's thirsty and really wants a drink! Where can she find water? Maybe she can go to a water fountain. Maybe she can go to her kitchen sink.

People use water every day. We drink water. We use water to stay clean. But where does water come from? How can we *describe*, or talk about, different types of water?

Can you see land on the other side of this ocean?

We find water in nature. Let us visit some natural sources of water.

First, we will visit an ocean. An ocean is a large body of salt water. If you have ever been to a beach, you have likely seen an ocean. Oceans are very large. Most of Earth's water is in oceans. About three-fourths of Earth is covered in water. Almost all of this water is salt water. Remember that Earth's oceans and seas contain salt water.

What Do You Think?

Some water is fresh water.

Water that is not salt water is called *fresh water*. People and many animals cannot drink salt water. They must drink fresh water. Very little of all water on Earth is fresh water.

Next, we will visit a *lake*. A lake is much smaller than an ocean. A lake has land all around it. At many lakes, you can see land on the other side. That's not true of an ocean! Most lakes are made of fresh water.

STEMscopedia

Not all lakes contain fresh water, though. Some lakes are full of salt water. China has many saltwater lakes. The United States has one of the most famous ones. Salt Lake City in Utah is named after its nearby Great Salt Lake. The lake is saltier than Earth's oceans! Salt collects on the shores of the Great Salt Lake in Utah. The lake gets very little rain. Three rivers feed into it, and there is no outlet. The lake is in a hot climate. Why would these conditions make it salty? The heat causes the water to evaporate and leave the salt behind, making it saltier and saltier!

What Do You Think?

Where do oceans and lakes get water? The water comes from rivers and streams. A *river* is a body of fresh water. It flows along land into a lake or an ocean. When you cross a long bridge, look down! You may see a river. That river takes water to a lake or an ocean.

A *stream* is also a body of fresh water. A stream is smaller than a river. Streams carry water into rivers. Next time you are hiking, listen for moving water. You may find a stream!

Fresh water comes from other sources.

It can come from underground lakes and streams. People can bring it up to the surface by drilling into the ground and building a well to bring up the water. Rain also provides fresh water. It runs off Earth's surface and fills rivers, streams, and lakes. However, pollution of freshwater sources has become an alarming problem facing our world.

STEMscopedia

Water is not only found on Earth as a liquid.

Look at the picture to the left. What states of matter do you see in this photo? The ocean water is a liquid. We have already discussed where water is found as a liquid. Do you see the glacier in the picture? The glacier is made of frozen water. There are also smaller floating pieces of ice. The glacier and the floating ice pieces are examples of water as a solid.

Other forms of water include hail, snow, and frozen lakes. All these sources of water are solid. When the temperature rises, the frozen water can be changed back into liquid water. Can you think of other sources of water?

Snow is water vapor that freezes and falls to the ground.

Hail is frozen raindrops that fall to the ground. They are larger than snowflakes.

This fresh water is frozen in a glacier (huge sheet of ice).

These people are ice-skating on a frozen lake.

STEMscopedia

Water Bodies Project

This project can help your child better appreciate local water bodies. First, visit one or more lakes, streams, oceans, or other water bodies near where you live. (You may also visit man-made water bodies, such as reservoirs, but be sure to explain to your child that people created these particular water bodies to meet their need for fresh water or their desire for recreation.) If you do not live close enough to a water body to easily visit it, conduct online research on a nearby water body. Your child should be able to describe the water (fresh or salt), as well as the kinds of organisms that live in or around the water body.

Encourage your child to learn how people in the community use the water body. If the water is fresh, do people drink it? Do people use it for bathing or cooking? If the water is salty, do people swim in it? Do they catch fish in it?

At home, instruct your child to make a postcard describing the water body for people who might want to visit it. The postcard should clearly identify whether the water body is a lake, stream, pond, or some other type of water body as well as if it is freshwater or saltwater. Your child should include illustrations of the water body and of any organisms that live nearby. The illustrations should also show how people use the water body.

Here are some questions to discuss with your child:

1. How do people in our community use this water body?

2. Why is the water in this water body useful for these purposes?

3. Has our community had to address problems with the water body, such as pollution or overuse? If so, how have we attempted to solve these problems?

Properties and States of Matter

STEMscopedia

Reflect

What is the difference between snow and water? Think about holding a snowball. A snowball feels cold. It is solid to the touch. You can change its shape by squishing it in your hands.

Water is a bit different from the snowball. It can be hot or cold, and it feels wet. If you spill water on your desk, it will flow and form a puddle.

We have seen how snow and liquid water are different. What are some things that are similar to snow? Can you think of other things that are similar to water? Why do scientists need to be able to compare things in this way?

Physical Properties of Matter

Mass

Flexibility

Texture

Temperature

Shape

Objects are made up of matter.

Matter is anything that has mass and takes up space. Snow is matter. Water is matter. You are matter! In fact, everything on Earth is made up of matter.

Our senses give us information about matter. You can see some matter with your eyes and touch some matter with your fingers. We can use this information to classify matter. When we classify things, we group them based on their similarities and differences.

We classify things based on their physical properties.

STEMscopedia

Matter has physical properties we can describe.

Physical properties include how something looks, feels, sounds, tastes, and smells. We have already described some properties of snowballs and water. Snowballs are cold and solid. Water is wet and can pour easily.

Let's review more properties of matter.

- **Shape:** Objects have different *shapes*. For example, a shoe box is shaped like a rectangular prism. A baseball is shaped like a sphere. Look at the objects and the captions below. How are a globe and a baseball similar?

| A pyramid is shaped like a triangle. | A globe is shaped like a sphere. | A toy is shaped like a cube. |

STEMscopedia

- **Mass**: The amount of matter in an object is its *mass*. If an object has a large amount of mass, it is usually heavy. If an object has little mass, it is usually light.

A bowling ball and a balloon are about the same size and shape. Which object has more mass? Think about how easy they are to pick up. The bowling ball feels heavier, right? It has more mass than the balloon.

- **Temperature:** *Temperature* measures how hot or cold something is. An object's temperature can change. The temperature of the air outside changes with the seasons. When does it feel cold? When does it feel hot?

Lava is hot.

Snow is cold.

- **Texture:** *Texture* is what an object feels like. Sandpaper has a rough texture. Glass has a smooth texture. A cotton shirt is soft, while some rocks are hard.

- **Flexibility:** *Flexible* objects bend easily. Some flexible objects will bend and stay that way. Other objects return to their original shape.

We can use physical properties to classify matter.

Remember that *classifying* means grouping objects together based on their properties. Think about chocolate. There are different types of chocolate. It can be sweet or bitter. It can be solid or liquid. It can be light or dark in color. Those are all properties we use to describe, or talk about, different types of chocolate.

These springs are flexible. They bend and return to their original shape.

 **STEMscopedia**

We can classify matter as a solid or liquid based on its properties.

A *solid* object keeps its shape. This is a property. A *liquid* takes the shape of its container. That is another property.

We classify these chocolates as solids. Some are light in color and some are dark, but all the chocolates hold their own shape at this temperature.

We classify chocolate milk with other liquids. Like water, it is wet and takes the shape of its container when poured.

Some objects can change from a solid to a liquid. When an ice cube becomes hot, it *melts*. The solid ice becomes liquid water. Objects can also change from a liquid to a solid. When water becomes cold, it *freezes*, and the liquid water becomes solid ice. As the properties of water change, the water looks and feels different.

Scientists classify objects to make it easier to study them.

For example, different types of rocks have different properties. Astronauts found rocks on the Moon. These rocks were dark and had many holes. Scientists used these properties to classify the rocks as basalt. Basalt is made from cooled lava. This observation told scientists that lava once flowed on the Moon. The basalt was evidence that there used to be volcanos on the Moon. Scientists plan and conduct investigations to discover new things about the world around them. They rely on the properties of matter to help them compare an object they know a lot about with one they have just discovered. How the objects are the same or different helps scientists make new discoveries.

STEMscopedia

Everyday Life: What's to drink?

Classification is useful in everyday life, too. When you are thirsty, you want something to drink. Look at the table below. What would you choose?

Soda	Juice	Water	Milk
Liquid	Liquid	Liquid	Liquid
Sweet	Sweet	Not sweet	Can be sweet
Little nutrients	Lots of nutrients	No nutrients	Lots of nutrients
Little fat	No fat	No fat	Can be high in fat

There are different types of drinks. Soda is sweet. Juice is also sweet, but it has more **nutrients**. Water is not sweet, and it is clear. Milk is white. Milk has nutrients, but it also has fat in it.

> **nutrients**: things that keep you healthy

All these liquids have different properties. Depending on what your body needs, the different properties help you decide what to drink when you are thirsty.

Classifying Matter

Children learn to classify objects at an early age. As they grow older and their vocabulary expands, their classifications become more complex and refined.

Take a trip with your child to a local natural history or science museum with a dinosaur exhibit. Start by reviewing a map of the museum with your child. Discuss the different classifications of artifacts in the museum, using the map as a reference. You might ask:

- Why are the dinosaurs in a different area than the other animals? *(They have different properties. They look different or have different body parts than other animals in the museum.)*

- Walk to the dinosaur area of the museum. While viewing the dinosaur exhibits with your child, ask questions about the relationship between physical properties and the process of classification. For example:

  - **Did all dinosaurs move around in the same way? (Some dinosaurs flew, while others walked.)**

  - **Looking at the dinosaurs in the exhibit, which dinosaurs can be classified as walkers or fliers? What characteristics are used to make this classification? (Walkers have legs, while fliers have wings.)**

The dinosaur exhibition exercise reinforces the idea of classifying objects based on their physical appearances and uses. Reinforce the concept of the physical properties of matter by finding a "touch-and-feel" or "fossil dig" area of the museum. If the museum lacks a hands-on fossil activity area, find a dinosaur fossil that is relatively close for observation. *(Don't touch the fossil unless the museum allows you to.)*

Discussion questions may include:

- What are the physical properties of the fossil?

(Answers may include solid, smooth or rough texture, descriptions of the fossil's shape, etc.)

Properties of Materials

Reflect

What properties does your pencil have that makes it easier for you to write? What makes a pencil easy to hold? You are probably thinking that a pencil is hard and thin. This makes it easier to use when writing on paper. What if your pencil was made out of rubber, like an eraser, and was very thick? Would this make it easier or more difficult to write?

Materials have properties that are used for different purposes. Unlike your pencil, a tire on a car needs to be *flexible*, which means it can bend easily. Hard tires would make a car ride very bumpy and rough!

Can you think of properties of your bed that make it comfortable for sleeping?

Objects have properties.

Knowing and understanding an object's properties can help us decide how to use it. Objects that are flexible are best used for making things bounce or roll. Objects that are very heavy might be best used to hold something in place. These are just a few examples of how an object's properties help us decide how to use it.

We classify things according to their physical properties. For example, some rocks are rough, while others are smooth. They have different textures.

STEMscopedia

Physical Properties of Matter

Some physical properties describe an object's flexibility. A flexible object is one that can bend. Other physical properties include size, shape, color, texture, and whether it can absorb liquid.

Properties of a Shoe

Look at the picture of a pair of shoes. Which property from the table describes how shoes are good for walking? Are there more than one?

Property	Description
Color	Brown
Size	7
Shape	Oval on bottom
Flexibility	Bendable
Texture	Soft, smooth

Since shoes are bendable, they are able to move with a person's feet. Other properties that are important are shape and size. If the shoes do not fit the shape or size of someone's foot, it would make walking more difficult. The color and texture are less important properties.

 STEMscopedia

What tools or tests can you use to measure or observe matter?

Physical properties can be observed and measured. Size, color, and shape are properties that can be observed by using your senses. Measurements made with tools can be used to describe other physical properties of matter. Let's take a closer look at some other properties of matter.

- You can compare objects by using their *weight*. Weight refers to how heavy or light something is. If someone held a baseball in one hand and a golf ball in the other, they could compare both objects. The baseball is heavier than the golf ball. It would be more difficult to hit a baseball using a golf club, and it wouldn't travel as far as a golf ball would. Look at the chart below to see other objects that are heavy or light.

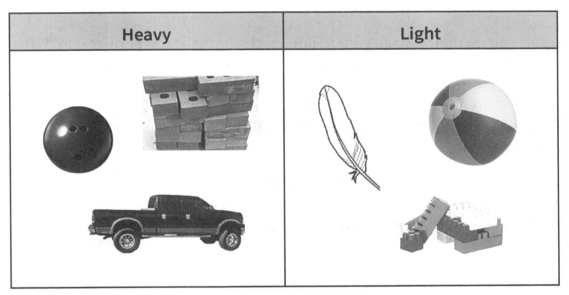

Heavy	Light

 **STEMscopedia**

- *Length* is the distance from one end of something to the other. When we compare objects by using length, we describe them as *long* or *short*. Let's pretend a ball rolled under the fridge. Would you need an object that is short or long to help you reach the ball? The length of an object can be measured using a ruler. Look at the toy car and the pencil below. The toy car is short and the pencil is long.

 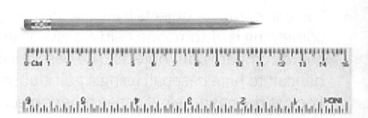

Using a ruler can be tricky! Make sure to line up the items at the correct end of the ruler. To get an accurate measurement, scientists carefully line up the item at the end of the ruler.

- *Texture* is what an object feels like. Sandpaper has a rough texture. Glass has a smooth texture. A cotton shirt is soft, while some rocks are hard.

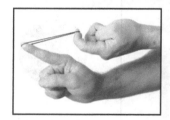

- *Flexibility* describes an object's ability to bend. Flexible objects bend easily. Some flexible objects will bend and stay that way. Other objects can return to their original shape.

Rubber bands are flexible. They bend and return to their original shape.

STEMscopedia

The properties an object has can help us decide how to use it.

For example, different types of shoes are used for different purposes. Think back to the properties that were used to describe the sneakers on page 2. What differences do you notice about the types of shoes in the pictures below? How do the properties of these two types of shoes affect how they are used in real life?

STEMscopedia

Reviewing Physical Properties at Home

Your child has learned about many physical properties of matter: size, mass, shape, color, texture, flexibility, physical state, magnetism, relative density (whether the object sinks or floats), and temperature.

Your child should be able to define and give examples of each of these terms. He or she should also be able to explain how to observe and measure each property. Given the appropriate tools—for example, a balance to measure mass, a ruler to measure length, a beaker to measure density, and a thermometer to measure temperature—your child should be able to measure each property.

Take your child on a tour of a specific location, such as a park or a playground. You may also explore a room of your home. As your child explores, he or she should identify each object in sight and describe that object, using as many physical properties as possible. If possible, bring a magnet, a balance, and other tools so that your child can include specific measurements as part of the descriptions. Monitor your child closely to make sure that he or she explores safely and does not touch anything that may be dangerous. If your child is unable to measure a property directly, ask your child to predict it. Try to confirm each prediction later.

Encourage your child to create flash cards of each object and property measured. He or she can use these flash cards as study aids.

Here are some questions to discuss with your child:

1. Which of these objects has more mass? Which of these objects has less mass?

2. Which properties of matter can you observe by using only your senses? Which properties do you need tools to measure?

3. Do you think that this object sinks or floats? How could you test this?

4. What is the difference in temperature between the hottest and the coolest?

5. Can you group objects that share properties? How many groups can you make?

Building Blocks of Matter

STEMscopedia

Reflect

Think about cars you see everyday. Do they all look exactly the same?

Cars are made up of many different parts. While most of the parts on cars are similar, they can be arranged, shaped, and painted to make each car look different from another one on the road.

Objects are made up of parts. An object can be made of different materials, or of smaller pieces of the same material. A fence could be built from a lot of wooden planks. The wall of a house could be built from many bricks. Everything we make, such as houses, clothes, and cars, can be made from objects found in nature. The properties of the objects we build help determine what we make them out of. We want cars to be tough and strong, so we make them out of metal. We want clothes to be flexible and soft, so we make them out of cotton or other soft, flexible materials.

Look around your classroom. Find an object that is made up of several parts. Think about how you could take the object apart and make it into something brand-new!

Look Out!

Observing Matter

All matter is made up of smaller parts. Jeans are made of cotton cloth. The cloth is made of cotton thread. The thread is made of very small pieces of cotton. These pieces of cotton are made of even smaller parts, which are too small to see without a microscope.

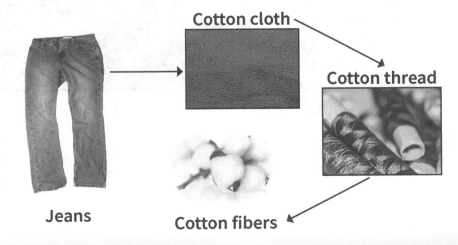

Cotton cloth

Cotton thread

Jeans

Cotton fibers

STEMscopedia

Do you like to play with blocks? How about your friends? When you play with blocks, you are acting like a scientist. When you stack the blocks, you are exploring balance and shape. When you build a road or a building, you are creating a model. When they all fall down, you are seeing gravity in action!

Have you ever tried to build a simple tower, only to have it fall down? You may have tried different ways of placing the blocks. Finally, you created a tower that stayed up! The tumbling tower was a problem you needed to solve. You explored what could be causing the problem, and you fixed it! You arranged small parts to make a larger object to solve a problem.

Many different objects can be built from a small set of pieces, such as blocks or building bricks. An object made of a set of small pieces can be taken apart and made into a new object multiple times.

You can build a house with building blocks. You can disassemble it and make a new object, using the same blocks.

You can build a castle with blocks. You can disassemble it and make a new object, using the same blocks.

STEMscopedia

Building Blocks of Matter

Ask your child to share knowledge about objects and their parts. Your child should share that an object is made up of smaller parts and can be taken apart and put together in a new way to make a different object.

Take a walk around your house. Find an object with several parts that can be taken apart— LEGO bricks or building blocks would work great. Take a picture of the object. Then, ask your child to take the object apart. Study all the pieces. Challenge your child to put the pieces back together in a new way, if possible. Take a picture of the reassembled object.

Here are some questions to discuss with your child:

1. How many parts make up the object?

2. Could the parts be assembled in a new way to make a different-looking object?

3. How did the appearance of the object change?

4. What stayed the same from the first assembly to the second assembly of the object?

Changes from Heat

 **STEMscopedia**

Reflect

Sometimes you feel too hot. Sometimes you feel too cold. How do you cool off? How do you warm up?

The fire gives the boys heat.

The fan cools the girl.

Take another look at these pictures. How does the fire change the wood? How does the fire change the food? How else can heat change things?

Adding heat causes changes to happen. What happens if you add heat to ice? The ice *melts*. It changes from a solid to a liquid.

Heat melts ice cubes. The solid ice changes to liquid water.

Adding heat also changes texture. *Texture* is how rough or smooth something feels. Ice may be bumpy or rough. Adding heat melts the edges and creates smooth water.

STEMscopedia

Heat changes things in other ways, too. In the examples below, we can see that heat changes the *color*, *size*, and *shape* of other objects. How did heat change these things?

The burner changed color.	The popcorn changed size.	The candy changed shape and state of matter.

Some changes from heat are reversible.

Once the burner cools down, the color will change back to black. When heat is taken away from the chocolate, it will return to a solid. However, the shape will not be the same as before. We call these changes *reversible*. Below are some more examples of reversible changes.

Butter can change back to a solid after heat is removed.			Melted ice cream can be changed back to a solid in the freezer.

Some changes from heat are not reversible.

Look at the popcorn in the picture above. Even if we were to cool the popcorn, it would not turn back into kernels. We call this change *irreversible*. Here are some more examples of irreversible changes.

Muffins cannot change back to liquid after heat is added.			Eggs that have been heated cannot change back to a liquid.

STEMscopedia

When we cool something, we take away heat. Water freezes when heat is removed.

Cooling changes things. Taking away heat *freezes* liquids. When a liquid freezes, it becomes a solid. Freezing gives liquids a shape.

How else can cooling change things? Red-hot objects are not red after they cool. Also, removing heat from water can make ice cubes with rough edges. That means cooling something can change its shape and texture.

Cream mixed with sugar is runny. It turns into solid ice cream when it cools.

The man is making a horseshoe. It will turn black when it cools.

Some changes from cooling are reversible.

If heat is added to the ice cream, it will melt and look as it did before it was cooled. Another example is Popsicles. After the juice is cooled, it turns to ice to form a Popsicle. It can then be changed back into liquid juice when heat is added.

Some changes from cooling are irreversible.

Sometimes it gets very cold outside, which causes a plant to freeze. The plant is not the same after it has been frozen. It cannot go back to the way it was before.

 **STEMscopedia**

Heat and Air

In this investigation, you and your child will study the way that air can expand and contract when heat is added or removed. You will need these materials: an empty, plastic water or soda bottle (about 1 pint); a refrigerator freezer; and a hot-water tap. The less rigid the bottle is, the better.

Begin by explaining that the empty bottle is not really empty, because it is full of air. Explain that air is made of extremely small, moving particles. As these particles are heated, they move faster. As they are cooled, they slow down.

Follow this procedure to complete the investigation:

- Put the cap on the bottle, and ask your child to squeeze it. Your child won't be able to crush the bottle, because it is full of air.

- With the cap still on, turn on the hot-water tap and hold the bottle under it for 1 minute. Ask your child to try to squeeze the bottle again. It will be even harder to squeeze the bottle, because the air inside expands when you add heat to it. (That is, the particles move more quickly and, therefore, are farther apart.) For further proof, undo the cap and listen to the air rushing out.

  - Put the cap back on the bottle, and put the bottle in the freezer. Ask your child to predict what will happen to the bottle in the freezer.

  - Remove the bottle after 30 minutes, and ask your child to explain why it changed shape. (Air contracts when heat is removed. The particles slow down, and, therefore, they cannot move as far apart.)

  - Finally, have your child hold out his or her hands, palms up. Explain that you are going to pour cold air onto them. Remove the bottle cap and tip the bottle as you would when pouring water into someone's hands. Your child will feel the cold air on his or her palms. Explain that you were able to "pour" the air because cold air is heavier than warm air.

Here are some questions to discuss with your child:

1. Can you name something else that changes size when heat is added or removed?

2. What do you think would happen if we filled the bottle with water and put it in the freezer? (Explain that water, like air, is made up of extremely small, moving particles. Although things usually shrink when they cool, water is unique in that the particles align to make a larger volume overall when it becomes solid. This is more detail than you need to provide to your child, but you can discuss that water is different from other materials for that reason.)

Quick Changes to Land

STEMscopedia

Reflect

The Big Island of Hawaii is the largest of the Hawaiian Islands. It is home to a very active volcano. The Kilauea volcano has been active since 1983. The lava that flows from the Kilauea volcano has added 500 acres of new land to the island.

Adding land from cooling lava can be good. The new area of land makes more space for plants and animals to live. However, hot lava from volcanoes can also destroy the habitat that was already there.

Volcanoes are not the only powerful force that can quickly change Earth's surface. Earthquakes and landslides can move land to new locations in a short amount of time. What happens when strong forces change the land very quickly?

Slow-moving lava from the Kilauea volcano hardens as it flows across the land and cools.

Look Out!

How do landslides change Earth's surface?

The movement of rocks under the surface of Earth causes earthquakes and volcanoes. Other changes to Earth's surface are easier to spot. Landslides happen when land moves over the surface of Earth.

Landslides happen when a big section of the ground suddenly falls or slips. Some landslides are caused by soil absorbing water. The wet dirt becomes heavy and collapses. Other times, earthquakes can cause landslides.

What Do You Think?

How do volcanoes change Earth's surface?

Powerful forces, such as volcanoes, act on the land. They can bring quick changes to the Earth's surface. In 1980, Mount St. Helens erupted in Washington State. The volcano's blast was powerful. It created a big crater that was 2 miles wide. The top of the volcano was lost in the eruption. Look at the before and after pictures. What differences do you see?

Volcanoes allow melted underground rock to reach the surface. Under Earth's surface, this liquid rock is called *magma*. When magma reaches the surface, it is called *lava*. When lava erupts quickly, it can change large areas of land. Over time, the lava cools and forms new rock and soil.

Look Out!

How do earthquakes change Earth's surface?

Earthquakes are another powerful force. Big chunks of Earth's surface move past each other. Sometimes they get stuck. After a while, they snap back in place. This sudden movement can cause the ground to shake. We call these sudden movements *earthquakes*.

Earthquakes can cause a great amount of damage. In 1906, a large earthquake hit San Francisco, California. The earthquake lasted only about a minute, but it caused large cracks to appear in the ground. Many buildings were destroyed.

STEMscopedia

Observing Changes to Earth's Surface

Some changes to Earth's surface happen very quickly (e.g., landslides, earthquakes, and volcanic eruptions), while other changes are very slow (e.g., mountain building and the shifting of continents). Scientists use different kinds of evidence to determine if a change to Earth's surface has occurred and, if it has, what kind of change it is. They can use direct observation of changes happening on Earth's surface or indirect observation with evidence that shows whether a change has happened. Help your child learn the difference between direct and indirect observation with the following activities.

What's the weather like?

Ask your child what the weather is like outside. How do they know? The easiest way is to look outside. This is direct observation; your child sees and feels what the weather is like. What if they could not go outside? How would they find out then? One way would be to observe how others who have been outside are dressed. Are they wearing shorts and a hat? If so, it must be sunny and warm outside. Do they have an umbrella? If so, it must be rainy out. These are indirect observations; your child is observing the effects of the weather on other things (what people wear).

STEMscopedia

What's happened to Earth's surface?

Give your child a piece of paper and a pencil and have them make a table similar to the one below, but with more blank space. Brainstorm types of direct and indirect evidence that would allow your child to conclude that an earthquake, volcanic eruption, or landslide has occurred. Performing an internet search to look at before and after pictures of each type will help your child come up with different ideas for indirect observations. Also, watching videos of each type of event will help them discover types of direct observations.

Change to Earth's Surface	Direct Observation	Indirect Observation
Earthquake		
Volcanic eruption		
Landslide		

Some questions you can discuss with your child include the following:

1. What is the difference between direct and indirect observations or evidence?

2. Were any of the observations (direct or indirect) the same for the different events? (For example, *ground shaking* could be listed under *Direct Observation* for both earthquakes and volcanic eruptions.)

3. Could you identify the type of change to Earth's surface if you were given only one piece of evidence, or would you need several different pieces of evidence?

Slow Changes to Land

 **STEMscopedia**

Reflect

Have you ever seen a sculpture that has been outside for many years? If the sculpture is of a person, the nose and mouth might be worn down. The face might have cracks in some places. The way the sculpture looks now is not how it looked when it was made. Think of the Sphinx in Egypt. Scientists think this sculpture was made around 4,500 years ago. After thousands of years, some parts of the Sphinx have worn away.

> **landforms**: Features on the surface of Earth, such as mountains

Earth's **landforms** change over time, too. Mountains are tall with steep slopes. They have sharp, jagged peaks. Over time, their slopes will become less sharp. Their peaks will become rounded and smooth, just like the face of the Sphinx. What forces in nature cause slow changes? How do you think these changes happen?

What makes these changes happen?

One way that landforms change over time is by weathering. Weathering happens when rocks break into smaller pieces. Think of the tiny grains of sand on a beach. Those grains of sand used to be parts of larger rocks or shells. Over time, pieces of the larger rocks or shells broke off. The pieces became smaller and smaller. Now they are just tiny grains. Different things cause weathering.

- *Wind* is one way that weathering can happen. Wind wears away tiny pieces of soil and rock called sediment. As wind blows against a mountain, the sediment grinds against it. This grinding action breaks off pieces of the mountain.

- *Water* can also cause weathering. Rivers carry sediment that grinds against the rock along the rivers' banks. Heavy rains also wear down rock. Over time, large formations, such as canyons, can form.

Weathering from water, ice, and wind helped create these natural arches in Utah. Over many years, parts of the rock were worn away, leaving empty spaces.

- *Ice* is solid water that expands when it freezes. If water gets into cracks in rocks and then freezes, the ice pushes the cracks. The cracks get wider. After melting and refreezing many times, the ice splits the rock into pieces.

STEMscopedia

Most rocks at the edge of a waterfall are rounded and smooth. Discuss with a partner:

- Why do you think the rocks are this way?

- What caused the weathering?

- Where else might you see how weathering has changed land?

Look Out!

Changes to land happen at different speeds. A volcano or an earthquake can change landforms in minutes! Wind, water, and ice take much longer to change the land. They cause small changes over time. It may take many years to notice these changes are happening!

Look at the tall, skinny towers of rock in the picture below. They formed from an area of rock that is 40–60 million years old. The rock is still changing today. Scientists predict that in another few million years, the rock towers will appear very different.

These towering rock formations are called *hoodoos*. Short, intense rainfalls are one agent that weathered and eroded the rock to form these structures.

What causes erosion?

Weathering is not the only way landforms change. When a rock breaks down into smaller pieces, these pieces are often moved. This movement of rock pieces to a new place is called erosion. Erosion is also caused by wind, water, or other natural agents.

Erosion and weathering are a little different. During weathering, rock surfaces are broken down by wind, water, and ice. During erosion, the pieces that were broken down are moved to a new location.

STEMscopedia

Weathering and erosion work together to change Earth's surface.

Things that cause weathering can also cause erosion. Wind causes erosion by carrying away loose sediment from landforms such as cliffs or sand dunes. In fact, sand dunes are constantly moving because of wind erosion. In the same way, flowing water carries away loose rocks and sand in a riverbed. Weathering breaks down rock into smaller pieces of sediment, while erosion carries sediment away.

Deposition creates new landforms, too.

Eventually, wind, water, and ice put down the sediment they carry. This is called deposition. Over time, the sediment builds up. Wind can carry sand. When the wind slows down enough, the sand falls to the ground. As more sand pieces collect, they may build new beaches and sand dunes. Rivers can carry sediment to a new body of water. Once the river water slows down, the sediment gets placed in a new location. The sediment creates new land at the mouth of a river, called a delta.

The Colorado River has weathered and eroded enough rock material over millions of years to create the Grand Canyon!

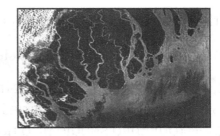

The picture above is the Ganges Delta in India, the largest delta in the world. Three rivers flow into this area and dump large amounts of sediments into the Bay of Bengal.

Like water and wind, ice can also cause weathering, erosion, and deposition. Glaciers are large sheets of ice that slowly move down mountains. They break off pieces of rock as they move. The glacier carries the rock pieces with it and eventually deposits them in a new location.

Weathering, erosion, and deposition are happening all over the world. They often happen at about the same time. These processes are so slow, it takes many years to notice a change in the land.

STEMscopedia

Changes Close to Home

To help your child learn more about changes to land, take him or her to a nearby park. If possible, choose a park with a variety of landforms and natural features, including rivers, waterfalls, hills, and boulders. Ask your child to identify as many landforms as possible.

Once the landforms have been identified, ask your child to hypothesize, or guess, how these landforms might have changed or caused change over time. (Your child has learned that wind, water, and ice cause changes to land.) Help your child write down his or her hypotheses in a small notebook.

Next, have your child safely explore the landforms more closely to look for evidence of change. Your child has learned about three types of changes to landforms:

- Weathering (rock breaking down into smaller particles)

- Erosion (the movement of rock particles)

- Deposition (the settling of rock particles)

For example, your child might note that the stones along a streambed are rounded and smooth. This is because the water carries small particles that grind down the rocks and make them smoother. Your child should also note whether the observations support or contradict his or her hypotheses about the landforms.

When you return home, research online the different landforms that you observed in the park. In particular, look for how they have changed or caused changes over time. Have your child compare his or her observations with the information found in the research.

Here are some questions to discuss with your child:

1. How have wind, water, and/or ice affected landforms in the park?

2. Did you see any signs of weathering, erosion, or deposition? If so, what kinds?

3. What are some human activities that might change the landforms in the park? How would these changes affect the plants and animals that live in the area?

Effects of Wind and Water

STEMscopedia

Weathering and *erosion* can change land and create interesting landforms, such as coastlines, mountains, and valleys. A famous landmark created by weathering is the Grand Canyon. However, some of the effects of weathering and erosion can be harmful.

Look Out!

One of the worst cases of erosion happened in the 1930s. It was called the Dust Bowl, and it happened in the Great Plains area. It included parts of Texas, Oklahoma, Kansas, New Mexico, and Colorado. Drought, too much farming, and high wind erosion were some of the reasons this large dust storm happened. The Dust Bowl put many farmers out of business. Animals and farming had destroyed the grasses in these areas. They could not grow crops, and there was nothing to hold the dirt to the ground. Many people had to wear masks before going outside. The masks would keep them from breathing in the dust particles.

The Dust Bowl destroyed millions of acres of crops.

How did they solve the Dust Bowl problem?

The government worried that the Great Plains would become a dry desert. They worked with farmers to come up with **solutions** to the erosion problem. Some companies tried to come up with ideas, such as covering the land with waterproof paper or trying to make it rain by firing a rocket in the air. Do you think those ideas would have worked? Why or why not? The government had to decide which solutions were good ideas and which were not.

solution: the answer to a problem

STEMscopedia

The government paid farmers to try soil conservation ideas. Farmers began planting trees to help block the wind. They also changed farming practices to make the soil useful for growing plants and crops again. Some learned how to pull water from below the ground instead of depending on rain. How would these ideas help with erosion?

Educating farmers on conserving soil helped many farms produce crops again. Some of these ideas are still used on farms today.

What Do You Think?

Scientists work to help prevent the harmful effects of erosion and weathering.

How can people prevent erosion?

Retaining Walls

Retaining walls are built using bricks or stones. They hold soil in and guard the soil against erosion from the wind. They are most often used in gardens. Retaining walls also control how water drains and flows in yards.

This retaining wall helps hold the soil in place.

Sandbag Barriers and Dune Fencing

You may have seen sandbags near a pond, river, or ocean. These bags are placed on the ground. They can be stacked to create a barrier. They are used to lessen the effects of water erosion. Water erosion can be caused by waves at the beach. It can also happen when rainwater fills a lake, pond, or river. Dune fences are used to help keep sand dunes from eroding away during high tide.

The dune fencing helps prevent water erosion.

STEMscopedia

Planting Trees and Plants

When new houses or buildings are built, bulldozers are used to clear the land. Trees and plants are knocked down. This makes room for the houses or buildings. New trees and bushes are planted to help replace the ones that were destroyed. New plants and trees help hold the soil in place. They protect the land against wind or water erosion.

Grass and trees keep the foundation under the house from eroding.

How can people prevent weathering?

Sealant and Paint

Mount Rushmore is checked daily for signs of weathering. You have learned that water can get into cracks. When it freezes, it can cause cracks to widen. To prevent damage to this important monument, sealant is added. The sealant keeps water from entering. This way, the cracks will not get large enough to cause the monument to fall apart.

Mount Rushmore is covered in sealant to preserve it.

STEMscopedia

To help your child learn more about ways people have tried to solve the problems of erosion and weathering, consider going on a walk or scavenger hunt around your neighborhood. Have your child look at the flower beds in different yards.

Next, have your child draw pictures of each of the solutions and, if possible, let your child look closely at each of the solutions they find (such as stones holding the soil in the flower bed).

1. Check to see if any dirt is spilling out of the flower bed.

2. Are the heights of the border stones the same?

3. How has this solution helped?

4. How could it be improved?

When you return home, help your child research online how to build a retaining wall using stones. Consider updating your landscaping to allow your child to experiment with different heights or configurations to prevent erosion of your own flower bed. Your child can use water to discover the most successful design.

Here are some questions to discuss with your child:

1. Where can you see ways people have tried to prevent erosion or weathering in your neighborhood?

2. Did everyone solve the problem of erosion in their flower beds the same way?

3. Which design works at controlling erosion the best?

What Plants Need

 **STEMscopedia**

How many kinds of plants can you think of?

Trees and grass are plants. So are bushes and shrubs. A plant is a living thing that makes its own food and cannot move from place to place on its own. Plants use their leaves to make their own food.

Some plants grow on land. Other plants grow in water. Maybe you have seen lily pads on a pond. The round, green pad is a leaf. The round leaves of water lilies float on the water. The rest of the plant is underwater.

What do plants need?

Plants need many things to stay alive. The most important things are water, air, and sunlight. Plants use these three things to make their own food.

Plants also need space. Big plants need more space than small plants. Some plants grow best in soil. Soil also holds water and helps keep plants upright and in place.

Lily pads are a type of plant that does not need soil to grow.

Caring for Plants

In spring many people plant new flowers in their yards. If they want their plants to grow, they have to take special care of them. What are some ways to make sure plants get what they need when they are planted?

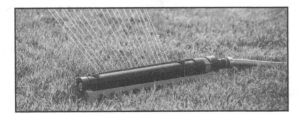

This sprinkler is a tool that sprays water on the plants and flowers in the yard.

These plants were planted with enough space to let each of them grow well.

STEMscopedia

What do plants need for growth?

Sunlight: Plants use energy from the Sun to make their own food. Not enough sunlight will slow down a plant's growth or even kill it. Too much sunlight can be a problem, too; it can make the soil dry out too quickly.

Water: Water comes from the sky as rain or snow. It flows on or through soil into lakes, rivers, and streams. Water is very important to plant growth. It helps the plant move nutrients from the soil up through its stems and leaves. Water keeps the plant moist and flexible and is needed for the plant to make its own food.

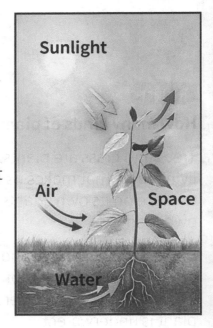

Look Out!

How much sunlight a plant gets is important.

A plant cannot make food if there is too little sunlight. It may stop growing and die. Too much sunlight may burn a plant's leaves.

How much water a plant gets is also important.

Too much water makes the leaves turn yellow and drop off. A plant without leaves cannot make food. Too little water makes a plant wilt. A wilted plant cannot make food, either.

This healthy plant got the right amount of sunlight and water.

This wilted plant did not get enough water.

Go Exploring with Your Child

To help your child learn more about the basic needs of plants, go on an exploration in your yard, a park, your neighborhood, or any other place that will provide the opportunity to observe a variety of plants. While keeping safety in mind, be creative with the habitat you choose, and invite your child to make suggestions for places to explore. You may go several times, exploring different habitats to find unique plants each time. Tell your child that you are searching for the strangest plants you can find. Before you go on the exploration, allow your child to help you brainstorm the types of plants you might see, such as trees, grasses, bushes, or shrubs.

During your exploration, have your child write down or draw a picture of plants that you observe and their parts. Then, ask your child to name the things the plants need to live. Ask your child questions, such as these:

1. What do plants need to make their food?

2. What do plants need to drink?

3. How do the roots help the plant?

4. How do the leaves help the plant?

If your child does not know the answers to these questions, you can take this opportunity to explain some of the plant's basic needs or to conduct internet research together when you return home. However, do not get too caught up in the verbal aspects of this activity; the physical exploration and observation will delight and fascinate your young one.

Here are some questions to discuss with your child:

1. What are plants?

2. Why do plants need sunlight, air, water, and space?

3. Where do plants get their food?

4. Why do plants need space to grow?

5. What do plants get from the soil?

6. How do you know a plant is a living thing?

Animals and Plant Dependence

STEMscopedia

Reflect

Different plants and animals live together. Look at the picture of the garden. What **organisms** live there? Grass, trees, bugs, and birds live there. Fish and frogs live there too. Can you think of anything else that might live there? How are these organisms important to one another?

Plants and animals depend on each other in many ways.

Animals need plants to live. Some animals eat plants. Other animals need trees for shelter to protect them from weather or other animals. Birds build nests in trees to protect their eggs from predators such as snakes.

organism: a living thing

pollinate: to transfer pollen from male to female parts of a plant to produce offspring

Most plants also depend on animals to live. Bees **pollinate** flowers. Without bees, many flowers could not make more flowers. Flowers produce seeds to make new plants.

To help their crops produce more food, farmers sometimes place beehives close to their fields. This makes sure there are plenty of bees to pollinate their crops.

Plants use their scent and color to attract insects and birds.

Look at the examples below. The bee is attracted to the nectar to make honey. Pollen has attached to its fuzzy body. Now the pollen can be taken to another plant to help new plants grow. When hummingbirds drink nectar from different flowers, they are also helping new plants grow.

Bees carry pollen from one flower to the next.

The hummingbird uses its long beak to drink nectar from the flower.

STEMscopedia

Plants also need to spread their seeds. This way, the young plants will have room to grow. Animals help plants spread seeds.

Plants attract animals by making fruit. When an animal eats fruit, it also eats the seeds inside the fruit. Then the animal moves somewhere else. The seed is dropped out in the animal's waste.

Some seeds have little hooks on them. These seeds stick to animals that pass by. When the seeds fall off the animal, new plants get to grow in a new spot.

People also help spread seeds by planting seeds. Some people plant flower and vegetable seeds in their gardens. Farmers plant seeds in their fields.

What Do You Think?

Can squirrels help spread seeds?

Squirrels eat nuts, which are seeds from trees. When a squirrel is looking for nuts for food, it moves the nut from where it fell to a new place. Sometimes the squirrel forgets a nut it has found. Sometimes it gets scared off and leaves the nut behind. This allows for more trees to grow.

Do all plants need animals to spread their seeds around?

Some plants, such as dandelions, use the wind to spread their seeds from one place to another. Other plants use gravity to help their seeds fall in a good area to grow in.

STEMscopedia

Pollination Around You

Pollination is an important process for plant reproduction. Plants depend on animals to help with this process. A bee, for example, uses its long, tube-shaped tongue to act like a straw. It sucks the nectar inside the flower. During this process, pieces of pollen stick to the tiny hairs on the bee. The bee then flies to a different flower to drink nectar again, and the pieces of pollen that are stuck to the bee fall off onto the new flower. Depending on where the pollen falls, pollination can occur, and a fruit and seed can be produced.

Take a walk with your child in your own backyard or even to your local park. Look around for flowers. Take a closer look at each flower, and ask your child to tell you about the parts of a flower. Wait and see if a bird or insect comes along to drink from the flower. Ask your child to think of other ways pollen can be transferred by different animals. Discuss what would happen if animals were to not help in the pollination process.

Diversity of Living Things

STEMscopedia

Earth is full of living things. It has many kinds of **organisms**, including bacteria, fungi (such as mushrooms), plants, and animals. There are many different kinds of living things in an area.

Have you ever gone into your backyard and noticed that there are many living organisms out there? Your backyard is its own **habitat**. You may have a tree where a family of squirrels lives. The tree could also be home to a family of blue jays. There are living and nonliving things in your backyard that help the tree survive every day. Your backyard is only one example of the many different habitats that exist on Earth.

habitat: where living and nonliving things interact and live

What are the parts of an environment?

organism: any living thing

Everything around an organism is part of its **environment**. Think about a tree. The dirt around the tree and the air around its leaves are a part of the tree's environment. Animals that climb on the tree and live on its branches are part of the environment too. Not every organism is able to survive in every habitat. A pine tree would not survive in an ocean!

How do the parts of an environment support life?

All organisms have needs. These needs must be met so the organism can survive. Air, water, food, and shelter are basic needs of animals. An environment provides its organisms with these basic needs.

environment: the living and nonliving things that are around an organism

Think about a forest habitat. The deer in the forest need air, which they get from their environment. The deer also need water, which they get from streams, rivers, or even snow in the winter! The trees provide shelter to help them hide from predators so they can survive. Deer need food, which they get by eating the plants in their environment. Can you think of a place where a deer could not survive?

What would happen if humans were to clear the forest for a shopping mall? Plants and animals would either have to move or not be able to survive.

STEMscopedia

Biodiversity is good for all habitats, whether they are on land or in the water. Each species that lives there helps keep things healthy.

> **biodiversity**: variety of plants and animals

Are all habitats the same?

Some elephants live in the African plains. Giraffes, lions, flamingos, gazelles, rhinos, and many plants also live there. Cows live on farms with grass and trees. Chickens, ducks, horses, dogs, and pigs also live there.

An ocean is very different from a farm or the African plains. Many different species of animals live in an ocean. There are sharks, fish, coral, dolphins, seals, seaweed, and pelicans that all depend on the ocean habitat to live. A lake is like an ocean, but the animals that live in that habitat could not survive in the ocean. How many different plants and animals can you think of that live in a lake?

STEMscopedia

Different kinds of living things live in different habitats.

Look at the two habitats below. Discuss with a partner how they are similar and how they are different.

Look Out!

Every habitat must be balanced.

There needs to be enough plants for animals to eat. There needs to be enough animals for predators to eat. If the habitat is not balanced, the organisms living there could die or grow too large for their environment.

Elephants eat over *300 pounds* of grass and bushes each day.

Bears sometimes eat 40 salmon in 1 day.

Connecting With Your Child

Build a Terrarium

Help your child learn more about the diversity of living things by building a terrarium. You can build a terrarium out of nearly any container. A clear container works best so that you and your child can more easily observe the interactions among the plants and animals. Suggestions for the container include a glass jar, water pitcher, aquarium, 2-liter soda bottle, or large, glass bowl.

STEMscopedia

Before beginning, you can take your child outside to observe parts of a local habitat, such as plants, dirt, and insects, or whatever you come across. Have your child make a list of all the things you will need to include in the terrarium to make a miniature habitat. As you make the list together, ask your child to explain why each item is being added to the list. Some items will be nonliving, so steer the conversation toward how these things are related to living things. For example, your child may say that soil should be included in the terrarium. Point out that soil is nonliving, and follow up by telling your child that animals such as earthworms add nutrients to the soil that are beneficial to plant growth. Your child may say rocks provide animals with shelter. Point out that logs and other parts of plants can provide shelter too.

After making your list, gather the materials with your child. It is best to build a terrarium with both plants and animals in order to see the diversity—how the living and nonliving things in your habitat depend on each other. Animals can include insects, worms, or small lizards. If necessary, conduct research to find out what the animals you include eat. You may decide to keep the terrarium for a very long time, but if not, be sure to come up with a plan for the living things before building the terrarium. For example, you might decide to replant the grasses outside in a garden and release native insects or earthworms back into the wild. Please remember that many animals, such as frogs, turtles, and lizards that are sold in pet stores, cannot be released into the wild. If you decide to use these kinds of animals, plan to keep them as pets for a very long time.

Make sure to have a conversation with your child about how biodiversity exists in different places on land and in water. The terrarium you build together is just one example of biodiversity.

Assemble the terrarium with your child. Allow your child to use creativity when putting it together, but emphasize the importance of building the terrarium so that the living things can interact best. This will show your child diversity in an environment. Ask questions such as the following: Are there enough leaves for the animals to have shelter? Is there food for the animals? Can air get into the container for the animals to breathe? Can plants get the gas (carbon dioxide) they need?

When completed, set the terrarium in a place where your child can visit it often and look at the different living things. Emphasize the importance of caring for the living things by making sure resources such as food and water remain available.

Here are some questions to discuss with your child:

1. Why does the terrarium need both plants and animals?
2. Why do the plants and animals in the terrarium need you?
3. How does the terrarium have biodiversity?

GLOSSARY OF TERMS

animal: a living thing that can move on its own and gets its energy from food; a living thing that cannot produce its own food

assemble: to put together the parts

bodies of water: ponds, lakes, oceans, and rivers

cooling: lowering in temperature; getting colder

design: a plan or drawing made to show how something should work or be made

disperse: to spread over a wide area

diversity: the different types of plants and animals in an area

Earth events: natural things that happen and change the shape of land

earthquake: a sudden release of energy under Earth's surface that makes the ground shake or crack

erosion: the gradual wearing down of something by wind, water, and other natural forces

evidence: information that supports an idea

form: the shape or nature of something

function: what something does

grow: increase in size

habitat: a place where animals or plants live

heat: the type of energy that makes things warm

ice: frozen water

intended purpose: what something is supposed to be used for

investigate: to gather information about a certain thing

irreversible: not able to be reversed

lake: freshwater surrounded by land

land: the solid part of the surface of Earth

liquid: material that can flow and drip

GLOSSARY OF TERMS

map: a drawing or picture that shows important things in an area

materials: equipment and supplies for doing or making something

matter: stuff that everything is made of

observable properties: the look, feel, taste, sound, or smell of an object

observe: to notice something with your senses; to use the senses to examine or inspect

ocean: a large body of water that is salty

physical model: a representation of something found in real life that you can touch

pieces: parts of a whole

plant: a type of living thing that gets its energy from the sun and is unable to move from place to place on its own; a living thing that can produce its own food

pollination: pollen being moved from plant to plant to produce seeds for future plants

pond: a small body of water with land all around it

problem: a situation that needs to be changed or needs an answer

property: a single part of the way something is

purpose: the reason that something is made

reversible: able to go through a change and then back to its original state (i.e., water to ice and back to water)

river: a body of freshwater that flows continuously toward the ocean

seed: a plant can grow from it

set: a group of things that go together

shape: the outline of something

solid: something that has a definite shape, such as a table or chairs; material that can be piled up

solution: an answer to a problem; the way to make a needed change

GLOSSARY OF TERMS

source: a place where something comes from

substance: something made of one material, such as water or copper

sunlight: the energy from the sun that plants need to make food

temperature: how hot or cold something is

time period: an amount of time, such as an hour, a day, a year, etc.

variety: different kinds of something

water: a liquid that all living things need to survive

weathering: when forces on earth break rocks apart or wear rock away

wind: moving air